SEASONS OF THE MOOSE

SEASONS OF THE
MOOSE

Text by
JENNIE PROMACK
Photographs and illustrations by
THOMAS J. SANKER

PEREGRINE SMITH BOOKS

SALT LAKE CITY

04 03 02 01 10 9 8 7 6

Published by
Gibbs Smith, Publisher
P.O. Box 667
Layton, UT 84041

Design by J. Scott Knudsen

Manufactured in Hong Kong

Library of Congress Cataloging-in-
Publication Data

Promack, Jennie.
Seasons of the moose / Jennie Promack &
Thomas J. Sanker
p.   cm.
ISBN 0-87905-455-7 (pbk.)
1. Moose. 2. Moose—Yellowstone National
Park Region. 3. Yellowstone National Park
Region. 4. Moose—Pictorial works. 5.
Moose—Yellowstone National Park Region—
Pictorial works. 6. Yellowstone National
Park Region—Pictorial works. I. Sanker,
Thomas J., 1949-   . II. Title.
QL737.U55P74 1992
599.73'57—dc20   91-36490
                                  CIP

This book is for Leidy and Rachel

CONTENTS

INTRODUCTION

The first time I saw moose I was taken by their appearance. They did not seem a part of this age. My impression was stirred as much by their massive size and distinctive silhouette as it was by their demeanor, the calm with which they moved and the intensity with which they looked at me. It is easy for me to imagine the moose of the Pleistocene, the ancestors of today's moose who crossed the Bering land bridge and expanded their range from the European and Asian continents into North America.

In the Ussuri Valley, on the Russo-Chinese border not far from the Sea of Japan, the earliest extant portrait of a moose was drawn on stone. The artist recreated the unmistakable profile and acknowledged the force within his subject with swirls and strong geometric patterns. Even then, the moose must have seemed ancient and mystifying.

Moose have a tremendous presence and people tend to react to them with fixed emotions based on a singular experience or the experiences of friends. These reactions are polarized; it seems that the moose is regarded as either a bumbling loner or a conniving aggressor. For instance, some people will tell you that a moose tried to kill them; some say that they know moose who are gentle as pets. Both are possible.

Moose lover or not, when one unexpectedly encounters a moose, one's first impulse is fear. An animal that causes us to stop and wonder at his intentions commands respect, and a mind open to understanding and possibilities.

Tom Sanker had been photographing moose for many years when we met; this book grew adjunct to our mutual admiration for moose. Moose are fearless, solitary . . . huge. To us, they are lords of the marsh.

Often, Tom and I meet before dawn. One drives while the other pours coffee. We talk moose. We head to the great Willows Flats, a few square miles of northwestern Wyoming, which provides the most accessible if not the finest place for moose watching.

From Memorial Day to the end of September, hundreds of tourists stop here daily. After photographs of the mountains or the obligatory family group shot with the Teton backdrop have been taken, the visitors linger to scan the flats for moose. Few know much about the animal, and those who do usually harbor misconceptions.

This book is a synthesis of scientific data yet also suggests what cannot be empirically known. My field observations were conducted at Willow Flats and throughout the Greater Yellowstone Ecosystem studying Shiras Moose. There are four subspecies existing in the lower forty-eight states. Whether living in Maine or Utah, moose have common behavior patterns.

At Willow Flats, Tom and I have repeatedly watched five splendid bulls and we identify them by name: Vincent, Carl, Herkimer, Albert and Victor. Herk was named by park rangers several years ago. Vincent has an obvious notch in his ear. Albert was named for his likeness to a moose painted by Albert Bierstadt. And Carl is named in honor of the great North American wildlife painter Carl Rungius. Collectively, we call them the boys. So far, their activity has been within the perimeter of accepted moose behavior. Their days of fighting, courting, basking and surviving continue to illustrate the balance and continuity of a moose's life.

We have also come to know an extraordinary orphan calf whom we named Annie. Annie's marked individuality exemplifies the "personalities" that exist within the moose tribe and her survival demonstrates the limitations of purely scientific interpretation. Her story is woven here.

In the beginning, I wanted more information about moose and so I read about them; but as I spent time among them, it became important to understand and interpret their behavior metaphorically as well as scientifically. With moose my education began.

Walk with moose, and when you go, hold science in one open hand and with the other reach for poetry.

PHOTOGRAPHER'S NOTES

Ten years ago in the Yellowstone backcountry, I stood motionless at the edge of the woods watching a moose and her newborn calf splash across a marsh twenty yards away. While the little calf, oblivious to my presence, struggled through the swamp trying to keep up with its mother, the cow moose watched me intently. She moved nervously but deliberately, her head lowered, not once taking her eyes off me.

The danger of the situation should have been obvious to me, but I missed her signals. Before I had read the meaning of her flattened ears and bristled withers, she had covered the distance between us in an explosion of water and fury. I swung around a tree just as the enraged moose slammed into it, then scrambled around on all fours ducking her wildly slashing hooves. With a contemptuous snort, she left me groveling there and returned to her startled calf. Although I have surprised grizzlies unexpectedly at close range and have been bluff-charged by black bears and bull elk, none of those animals put

The approach of a potential rival easily distracts a bull from feeding.

as much fear into me as that moose did. Hers was no threat. She meant to eliminate the perceived danger—to kill me.

That close encounter left an indelible impression; in a moment moose had gained my respect and attention. My ongoing fascination with these magnificent animals has led to this book. I took my first pictures of moose fifteen years ago in Maine and have since photographed them in eastern Canada, the Canadian Rockies, and throughout their range in the American West. The Yellowstone and Grand Teton ecosystem, with its spectacular scenery and diverse landscape, has become my favorite place to observe, sketch and photograph moose.

Photographing moose, or any wildlife, is a matter of going out there, into their habitat—in all kinds of weather—and applying hundreds of hours of patience. Getting good images has as much to do with luck as skill; but you have to be there. Luck is the reward that comes with persistence, some hardship, frustration, and plenty of disappointment.

I feel that photographic equipment is of secondary concern. There is a wide variety of camera makes and types that can produce good pictures. A telephoto lens serves to keep you out of harm's way and helps prevent your interfering with the natural behavior of animals. If you are in focus and have the proper exposure settings (there are cameras now that do all that for you), you could get a gorilla to release the shutter.

Paramount in successful wildlife photography, I think, is knowledge of the animal. Observation and study of wildlife behaviors and movements is indispensable. I have spent a great deal more time looking at moose through binoculars than through the viewfinder of a camera. I was fortunate to get to know some moose as individuals (especially Annie, the little orphan who captivated me with her antics and spunk), which helped greatly, as I became familiar with their routines and reactions to my presence.

I came to know that moose communicate their intent. I believe they think a situation through, weigh alternatives, and then act. I have watched them do this. It becomes important, then, to understand their language as best we can. I never approach moose directly, return a stare, or do anything that they may read as aggression.

I never forgot that I was an intruder, a visitor in the sanctum of the moose. I tried to act accordingly. Moose allowed me limited access to their realm, but always on their terms. I wouldn't have it any other way. For me, it will always be a privilege to go into the woods and be in the company of such extraordinary animals.

THOMAS J. SANKER

ACKNOWLEDGEMENTS

I am grateful to a number of people and institutions for assistance and support in writing this book.

The Teton Science School in Kelly, Wyoming, was a critical source for scientific information. I am grateful for the use of their library and for the generosity and resourcefulness of the staff.

Profound gratitude goes to Christopher Merrill, who gave encouragement, introduction and insight.

Bill and Joffa Kerr provided early direction that enabled me to establish a course; moreover, they believed it was important to tell Annie's extraordinary story.

I thank my brother Dean Krakel II, who first brought me to the high country, for providing intelligent professional considerations and for reading parts of the manuscript in progress. His support and faith were dearly gratifying, and I hope to honor him with this effort.

George Sanker, Jr., lent his professional expertise for business affairs, and his philosophical interpretation of nature has illuminated my path.

I would like to thank Jon Stuart and the staff at Mountain Camera Supply. I wish to thank Ken Wientjes and Ray Coleman at Unilink in Jackson, Wyoming, for their patience and assistance. They made house calls.

The National Park Service operating in Grand Teton National Park provided data that was important to my research. I particularly thank Bob "Sagebrush" De Groot, who first introduced Herkimer and was a friendly source of information about life in Willow Flats and surrounding areas.

Rick Konrad is a good friend and was a companion on several moose adventures. He was my eyes when I could not be north with the moose.

Stephen Ashley and the entire staff at Valley Bookstore in Jackson provided a sounding board toward the production of this book, encouragement, and refuge among the stacks. I am indebted.

At Wildlife of the American West Art Museum in Jackson, I found solace in the galleries and inspiration in the unconditional support of the staff. I especially thank Patti Boyd, whose friendship, insights and expertise were invaluable.

Good friends Jan and Marty Kruzich are great in spirit; their faith, combined with wisdom and humor, enabled me through difficult times.

Profound gratitude goes to Tom Sanker, who read every draft of the manuscript with an eye for truth and an ear for language. He is a blood brother. From his absolute confidence in me, I drew courage. On his behalf, I would like to thank Jane Macdonald, whose ebullient spirit was a tonic.

I would like to thank Gibbs and Cathy Smith of Peregrine Smith Books. I am particularly indebted to Madge Baird, who believed in our project. Through sensitive reading and skillful editing, she helped focus the manuscript.

Tom and I wish to thank our parents, Dean and Iris Krakel and George and Shorty Sanker, who established bedrock foundations of love from which we have drawn strength and inspiration. It is difficult to express how much their love means and the scope of our love for them. I am humbled by friends and family whose devotion made this book a reality. My heart is full.

COMMON THREADS

The moose is commonly believed to be a slow-witted, quick-tempered, clumsy animal with poor vision. His massive size, broadly palmated antlers and long muzzle have lent themselves to caricatures from the political cartoons of Teddy Roosevelt's Bull Moose Party in the years before World War I, to Bullwinkle. Although what we know of the moose may be limited to what we have seen on Saturday morning cartoons, the sight of these giants, like Pleistocene dreams, is powerful and mystifying. Moose are the world's mightiest antlered animal and North America's most exotic ungulate.

The moose is perfectly suited to life in the world's boreal forests and wetlands. With a circumpolar distribution, there are seven subspecies of moose, four of which live in North America:

The Eastern Moose (Alces alces americana) resides in the forests of eastern Canada from Nova Scotia and New Brunswick to the eastern parts of Ontario. This subspecies is found in Maine and has reestablished its range in other New England states and New York.

The Northwestern Moose (Alces alces andersoni) is found in northern Michigan and Minnesota, and western Ontario, extending

Whether living on the East Coast or in the Rocky Mountains, moose exhibit common behaviors.

west into central British Columbia and north to the eastern parts of the Yukon.

The Alaskan Moose (Alces alces gigas) lives in the western Yukon region, northwestern British Columbia and in the wooded regions of Alaska.

The Shiras Moose (Alces alces shirasi) is found primarily in northwestern Wyoming, Montana, eastern and northern Idaho, southern Alberta and southeastern British Columbia. Having extended its range, small populations of this subspecies are found in northern Utah and the Colorado Rockies.

The Alaskan Moose is 30 percent larger than the other subspecies inhabiting North America. With this exception, there are few differences among moose of this country. The easiest method of subspecies identification is geographical context.

Average bull moose weigh 1100 pounds. That is 300 pounds more than an average bull elk and 850 pounds more than an average white-tailed deer buck. They are nine feet from nose to tail, stand over six feet at their prominently humped withers and yet they appear and disappear among the willows and in and out of forests with the stealth of an apparition.

At a distance moose appear to be black. At close range, individuals are variously colored from burnt umber to chestnut to a silvery buff that resembles the hoary shoulders of a grizzly bear. The long, sculptural muzzle is somewhat lighter, particularly between the antler pedicels and around the mouth. The short hair on their lower legs and the insides of their hind legs to their buttocks is light gray. Their bellies are grayish tan as are the deep furry pockets of their ears. Over the hump and along the spine, the hide is an inch thick with a coarse mane that stands erect when the animal is angry or agitated. Moose hair is hollow. This helps keep them comfortable in extreme temperatures and perhaps more buoyant in water.

Moose have a short excuse for a tail, scarcely more than two or three inches long. When seen from the rear, their hindquarters are sharply angled and powerfully muscled. The forequarters are stationed higher than the hindquarters and resemble those of a well-toned Tennessee walker. Moose have mammoth shoulders and a massive neck from which hangs a bell, or dewlap, on both sexes.

The bell is unique to each animal and serves as a marker for identifying individuals. Some are short and blunt, others are long dangling appendages, while yet others may be forked, bladelike, or mere tufts of hair. The dewlap consists of skin and fur and serves no certain purpose. A moose may lose a portion of its dewlap to frostbite or damage it during rutting battles.

Moose have communicative brown eyes capable of soul-shaking, laserlike stares. Although their eyes seem small relative to the size of their great heads, their vision is keen. The pupils are elliptically shaped; therefore, sight may be somewhat limited on the vertical plane. However, the position of their eyes and the exceptional mobility of their eye muscles enable moose to see nearly 180 degrees horizontally. Moose can see all but what lies directly behind the axis of their bodies.

Their large ears provide acute hearing and are able to pivot independently in all directions. They flick and turn at the slightest sound. It has been suggested that the placement of ears and antlers may actually serve to amplify sounds for the bull moose.

Their sense of smell is highly developed and accentuated by generous tear-shaped nostrils. Good light and a close look reveals the shell pink interior of the nose. Moose determine much about an intruder through scent and may circle downwind for an informative sniff.

On their upper and lower jaws, moose have six premolars and six

A sound in the willows
captures the rapt attention
of a five-month-old calf.

molars. Like many other ruminants, they have no upper incisors, having instead a hard-ridged gum tissue called the premaxillary. Additionally, on the lower jaw, they have eight razor-sharp incisors. Their mouths are perfectly adapted to forage on shrubs and branches, which are the mainstay of their diet. This trait engendered the word moose, which was adopted by white settlers from Algonquin Indian dialects and means "he strips or eats off."

Their long overhanging upper lip is firm but velvety to the touch, with a small triangle of dark hair. The muscular, bright pink tongue is indifferent to the prickly thistles on which moose occasionally feed.

When eating ground cover, moose strike an awkward stance. They splay their long front legs and stretch their necks to the ground. Occasionally adult moose and frequently calves will kneel on their forelegs to eat or drink. Stretching their necks, moose can easily feed on the leaves of trees ten feet above the ground. By sliding their chins up the trunk of a sapling they are able to bend the tree and feed on leaves and succulent buds growing even higher. Moose chew food only a few times before swallowing; later, small amounts of partially digested material are regurgitated and chewed as cud. Moose are avid aquatic feeders relishing pondweed, water lilies and algae. Their prehensile upper lip is as strong and as sensitive as our fingertips. With it, they are able to feel for the tender roots and tubers of water plants. Often moose feed with their heads completely submerged.

Maneuvering through water with grace equal to their terrestrial movements, moose are able to swim effortlessly for two hours or more at a pace of about six miles per hour. They have been known to dive to depths of nearly twenty feet. In summer months, they spend hours feeding and cooling off in favorite ponds and backwaters.

Moose love the water.

Moose have split hooves that are sharply pointed and roughly six inches long. In mud or wet snow the imprint of two dewclaws may be visible. Both sexes use their hooves as weapons and kick with ferocity and precision.

The moose's antlers are perhaps its most physically impressive characteristic. Of all members of the deer family, moose have the largest, heaviest antlers. The headgear on a large Shiras bull may weigh fifty pounds or more and span fifty inches across. Antlers are grown through spring and summer, are used to demonstrate dominance and sexual prowess in fall, and are shed each winter. They consist of solid bone rich in calcium, phosphorous and mineral salts. From knobby pedicels on the skull above the eyes, the antler beam widens into a palm, or basin shape, from which long tines project.

The individual physical attributes of this animal may at first make it seem ungainly. But moose move with breathtaking fluidity and poise.

Snows mean persistent
searching for good forage.

Late-season estrus initiates a belated courtship.

Moose do not panic like other deer and thus they rarely run. Their movements are not instinctual reactions to fear but rather, seem to be studied maneuvers based on intelligence and common sense. When they choose to move quickly, moose usually favor a high-stepped bicycling trot. They can run through the forest at speeds up to thirty-five miles per hour. Whether the terrain is dense timber, deadfall, deep snow or wetland, the grace of their gait is unaffected.

An adult moose is not timid. It studies another animal without alarm. Although not generally antagonistic toward other species, the moose is able to defend itself well against predators such as wolves and grizzly bears. A cow with a calf or an enraged bull in rut is terror personified. In fact, even grizzly bears have been known to defer to a moose when the two meet on a trail.

In North America grizzly bears, wolves and mountain lions are the only natural predators of moose. As predator habitat and numbers dwindle, moose are much less likely to be killed through predation. The highest numbers of moose fatality are probably claimed by humans either with a gun or an automobile.

Much less social than other members of the deer tribe, moose do not congregate into distinct herds. Preferring solitude, their proximity to each other is usually the result of plentiful food supply; nevertheless, moose may be found together more commonly at certain times of the year. Bulls enjoy limited associations in early winter immediately following the rut. Cows raise their young until the calf is a year or two old and the birth of a new calf is imminent. During courtship and mating, the bull moose, cow and the cow's calf remain together for a week to ten days.

Moose employ a variety of vocalizations ranging from the bull's throaty, hollow grunts and tremendous bellowing sounds to the female's slightly higher-toned, wavering call. Cow moose also produce a short, raspy cough to attract the attention of their young; likewise, calves use successive barks to call their mothers.

Moose are not truly migratory as are caribou and elk. Typically, their winter and summer range may be only a mile in radius as long as food supply is ample. Living to an average age of fifteen years, moose may spend their entire lives within ten miles of their birth-place.

Science presents us with a clean package of knowledge. But it provides only a glint toward really understanding the moose. Every moose exhibits behaviors that are curiously singular, conscious and personal. These unpatterned and mysterious manifestations of their behavior can be the most compelling.

Moose are intelligent. They make choices. They command authority and we oblige. They require distance and we stay away. We have a huge lexicon yet cannot always say what we feel; they speak with their eyes or a tilt of their heads.

Moose are noble in power, mystery and beauty. Purely alive in the physical, wholly in the moment.

THE ORPHAN

Tom Sanker first saw the orphan one morning in midsummer. The light of early dawn tinged the mist with violet as Tom stood hunched and still, photographing a large bull moose browsing along a creek. The bull's antlers, not yet fully developed, were tender and rounded in velvet. After several minutes, the bull looked up and turned his gaze past Tom to a moose calf emerging timorously from the protection of willows one hundred yards away.

A cow moose is never far from her offspring. Her response toward a perceived predator can be acid quick and just as lethal; so the proximity of a fiercely protective mother added urgency to Tom's work.

The calf was tiny, hardly five weeks old by Tom's estimation. It was a tawny bay color with two black spots obscuring its eyes. The little moose furtively made its way through the meadow, alternately eyeing the big bull and the photographer, clearly more interested in the bull. Maintaining a careful distance of about thirty feet from the grazing bull the calf anxiously followed him to a nearby beaver pond. The moose calf stood in the shallow water along the pond's edge, where it watched the elder eat pondweed and drink.

Annie at six months.

When more than thirty minutes had elapsed with no sign of the calf's mother, Tom was sure that the calf was an orphan.

Finished with aquatic browsing, the bull climbed the slope above the pond. Following too closely, the calf unwittingly stumbled into what might be called the bull's margin of intolerable closeness. Head down and displaying his anger, the older moose rushed the orphan. Within a few minutes he charged again. This time, the baby retreated to the willows, where it slept. When the calf awoke the bull was gone. Tom watched the orphan for three hours that morning.

Later, Tom and I canvassed the area looking for the remains of the calf's mother. On an east-facing slope we found, instead, the body of another calf. We suspected that this was the orphan's twin, who had fallen prey to coyotes. The remains lay under a canopy of spruce trees and lodgepole pines, where they were cradled in fragrant pine needles and velvety alpine mosses. I was moved by the sight of the bones lying like so many bits of a broken necklace. Many of the little shapes were already clean and milky gray; only a foreleg and tiny arrow of foot remained intact. I was particularly touched by the vertebrae, so small that one would not have made a ring for my little finger. The memory of that place worked on me.

When we reported the orphan to park headquarters in Moose, Wyoming, the rangers said it would probably not survive a month, and if by some fluke it survived the summer, it surely would not live through the winter. We hated the finality of this logic, and each subsequent glimpse of the orphan kindled our hopes.

We began to look for her every time we went north to study moose. The calf became a blessed respite from the raw elemental strength of bulls in rut and bulls broken and thin from the rut, and from the sheer drudgery of slogging through marshes, where the willows invariably whip one's ears when least suspecting it. Seeing the orphan was always an unexpected gift. Its small, wedge-shaped head, two shining black eyes and mulish ears hailing skyward never failed to delight us. We joyfully measured the length of the calf's survival with each sighting.

One morning a young bull (too young to participate in or to be very interested in rutting) led the orphan from its secluded glade on Christian Creek, over a ridge and down into the expanse of the Willow Flats area. When the two moose emerged into the open, they leapt and bucked for joy. We hoped that the young bull would take the orphan under his wing, but the partnership was brief and soon the calf was back home, alone. Repeatedly, we spotted the calf feeding on the fringe of cow-and-calf groups. Invariably, the orphan was spurned and would return to her small L-shaped valley, where there was solace in familiarity.

The last week of October, a little more than three months since our discovery of the calf, Tom came back from the north with news. His exact words, "It's a girl . . . she looks fine." Inexplicably, our hearts enlarged to know that the orphan was a little girl. We didn't trust her survival more, but it added a dimension to the human framework in which we had come to know the calf. We tossed around names for her and unashamedly settled on Annie.

Annie was prettier than other moose calves, though it would gain her nothing. Her coat was glossy and darkening now. Her intelligence was obvious, her eyes larger, her ways more sweet.

Tom Sanker and I had become the self-appointed, powerless guardians of a wild untouchable child.

A bull's proximity to a new calf
is rare. Here the orphan
seeks companionship.

The six-week-old orphan in her meadow.

AUTUMN BEGINNINGS

In early September, Tom and I arrived at the Willow Flats area thirty minutes before there was enough light to see. We scanned the flats for black shapes against black. We listened as the eerie light of predawn was pierced by the otherworldly bugling of bull elk. Often, before we could see them, we heard the tempestuous thrashing of moose in the willows or the wooden-sounding clatter of antler hitting antler.

After eight nights of hard frost, the leaves of aspen and cottonwood trees changed from faded green to shimmering cadmium yellows and pomegranate. Fall is the ephemeral and poignant culmination of the moose year.

During autumn, the skills with which moose communicate and interpret are exemplary. Always moose are completely and utterly aware and in fall a powerful current charges their faculties. It is a thing known deeply yet not rationalized, a thing that urges their behavior and strengthens their knowledge without making itself known, that connects moose of this fall to moose on the Bering land bridge during Pleistocene times. It is the awesome ritual.

A bull gauges the proximity of a cow in estrus through an information-gathering behavior known as the Flehmen Response.

Now moose are in glorious physical condition. With their incessant summer feeding, bulls have added a full 15 percent to their average 1100-pound frames. Their dark, glossy coats reflect changing light and their muscles seem swollen with pride and burgeoning sexuality. Nothing in their demeanor portends the 20 percent weight loss which will occur during the rut.

As rut begins, their inexorable drive to procreate overwhelms even their desire to eat. With almost constant motion, bulls demonstrate their muscled prowess when charging rivals, bluffing would-be contenders, or displaying their mighty antlers in ritualistic posturing.

Within their characteristic movements of grace and deliberation the tension is palpable. One senses an elemental blast about to happen. The Willow Flats becomes a hushed theater whose curtain of tangled thickets hides an ancient and exhausting ritual in three acts: battle, courtship and mating.

Bulls congregate loosely in late summer, but as the moon waxes toward harvest, they begin to regard one another suspiciously and establish broad circular territories. The rut has begun.

For the Shiras moose, the rut begins about the second week of September and is, for the most part, over by the middle of November. Occasionally a cow may come into estrus and be bred even later. But the intense period of courtship and antler-crashing known as the rut is very brief.

An adult bull in his prime is a powerful and fearless animal. His mighty and cumbersome antlers are carried with monarchic arrogance. They are burnished and honed to perfection resulting in mahogany-colored palms and polished white tines.

In early September, triggered by decreasing sunlight and hyper-increased levels of testosterone, moose antlers harden to bone. The rich sheath of brownish-maroon velvet has fed the growing antler for seven months. The blood supply that nourishes the velvet abates and the velvet dies. As it dries, it turns black and peels, hanging like shredded fabric from the antlers.

Moose may experience some itchy discomfort while shedding velvet. To hasten the process and to exorcise their increasing irritability, moose part their pathways antler first. After these battles with brush, some antlers sport a rakish sprig of aspen, like a victor's wreath.

We watched a large bull vigorously rub his antlers against a sixteen-foot aspen tree. He angled his head and threaded the tree's branches through his tines and along the fluted palms. Periodically, he closed his eyes in apparent satisfaction. A cow watched this process attentively. She was visually attracted by the bull's antlers and by his scent. When he had satisfied his itch and all but destroyed the small tree, the moose cow rubbed her throat and face on the sapling for several minutes, possibly trying to bond the bull to her with his scent.

Scent is an important part of the mutual attraction between the cow and bull. Sometimes bulls will find or create a shallow depression in the ground, urinate and paw the earth until the depression is a pungent muddy mess. These wallows retain an evil stench for days. Cows who want to be bred will lie in the wallow, coating themselves with the pasty mixture of mud and urine.

The size and strength of moose belies the tenderness of their courtship.

Actual mounting is very brief and may occur several times before successful mating is achieved.

To prevent other cows from attracting the bull, a female may defend a wallow vigorously; cows kick each other, stomp and deal thwacking blows with the sides of their heads. Cows become extremely agitated, territorial and absolutely intolerant of each other when competing for good forage and the bull of their choice.

Mature moose cows produce a musky scent that is borne on the autumn breeze to any bull within a mile. Although they are sending potent sexual messages, cows forage continually throughout the rut. They will feed even when mating is imminent.

A bull moose is aware of a cow's presence long before he sees her. He stands with his chin lifted and neck fully elongated. He opens his mouth wide, as if to give a mighty bellow, but makes no sound. Common to many ruminants, this behavior is called the Flehmen Response. This behavior enables a biochemical reaction to take place in an olfactory gland located in the bull's palate. It is through the scent or taste of a moose cow's urine that a bull determines if she has ovulated.

When approaching females, bulls salivate copiously, chomping and lip-smacking with anticipation laid bare. They walk with steady purpose and emit a rhythmic, hollow gulping sound at about two-second intervals: gungh . . . gungh . . . gungh. This might last several seconds and, after a Flehmen Response, it begins again.

While deer and elk ruts are characterized by the massing of females into harems or herds, moose mating is a form of limited polygamy. A bull moose will breed with one cow and stay with her for a week to ten days before leaving to find another cow with whom to mate. Some moose seek the same mate year after year. Although personal attachment is within the scope of the moose psyche, it is more probable that this behavior occurs as a result of habitual movements inside overlapping territories. A dominant bull will usually mate three or four times during the rut.

Moose are solitary animals, and so it is absorbing to watch adults seek each other for courtship or battle. Their movements, whether blatant or subtle, are ritualistic and seem highly charged. Two bulls

may rub their antlers companionably, then suddenly assault each other with jolting ferocity.

We watched a venerable old fighter consent to spar with a young lightweight who had mere spades for antlers. During rut, immature moose study adult moose behavior and frequently imitate what they see. This young bull was learning the ropes with each nudge from an elder three times his age. Then suddenly impatient with mere play, the older bull thrust hard, sending the young bull stumbling into cover. A bull's reputation for a testy disposition and unpredictability is epitomized in the fall.

When bull moose spar antler to antler, it is not so much to legitimize their individual perceptions of territory as it is to agree, or not, on one bull's physical and mental preeminence. The combatants move to ancient orchestrations in ways that are remarkably deliberate and communicative. When a confrontation is brooding, bulls approach one another with a stiff-legged walk. They seem to gather their strength and hold it high in their shoulders, neck and head.

A thunderous clash between equally matched bulls.

They are acutely aware of everything around them; yet their eyes are molten and remain fixed on their adversary. They halt to stare at one another. So intense is the glare of an enraged bull, that often it is all that is needed to dissuade a confrontation. If the convictions of the two are fairly matched, they will initiate their ceremonious approach: one bull displays his antlers. Looking squarely ahead, he slowly pivots his mighty rack from side to side. Head down, he shows the curving girth of his palms. In response, the other bull will brandish his antlers wildly at the brush.

These acts of intimidation may preclude injurious battle. As the pioneer animal behaviorist Conrad Lorenz postulated, "Ritualization displays diffuse aggression and render conflict less dangerous between members of the same species." If neither contender is daunted by the other's performance, an explosive spectacle ensues.

With ears flattened and eyes riveted to eyes, the moose charge simultaneously and clash with thunderous impact. Their rear legs are flexed and firmly anchored; their weight is concentrated over their massive haunches before they lunge into their opponent. A mighty thrust can lift all forelegs off the ground and send the challenger stumbling backward. The bulls constantly circle and parry for stronger positions from which to torque and jab their tremendous antlers. Mouths open, they loudly expel air from their lungs. They jerk and lift their heads violently.

At the mutually accepted conclusion of the fight, both bulls bow to exhaustion. You can believe after watching bull moose in battle, that fights to the death do happen, but such vengeance is rare and does not serve the species. Confrontations repeated among the bulls over and over through the autumn are not just hormone-induced brawls. They are patterned exhibitions of strength and wit whose intent is rather like the Native American practice of counting coup. Still, by the end of October, bulls tell of their ordeals with cuts and lame feet and antlers sheared in half.

The elemental drama of rutting battles is beautifully juxtaposed with the cow's coquettish antics. She is in complete control. The surging bravado among the bulls is all for her benefit and she knows it.

Moose cows are enormously engrossed by battles which occur in their proximity. Yet, the loser of a confrontation may still be the one with whom the local cow chooses to mate. The female will pursue the male she wants, calling to him repeatedly. But bulls are exhausted for hours following a heavyweight bout, panting loudly and drinking deeply if they can. It is a wonder that there is any strength left in bulls for the ultimate task.

Cow moose are as mercurial as September weather. Early in the rut when trying to attract bulls, they are flagrantly demonstrative. Cows vocalize much more frequently than bulls. As they approach estrus, they call to males with urgent, plaintive sounds that begin in their bellies. With their sensitive muzzles, they stroke the sides of prospective swains and playfully touch and sniff the undersides of bulls' antlers.

Compared with other ungulates, courtship between a cow and bull moose is long and ritualistic. When the promenade begins, the bull is persistent while the cow is a portrait of sufferance. This behavior seems to push the already exhausted bull to the limits of his constraint. But the stirrings of sexual attraction are too compelling to ignore, despite the ostensibly fickle nature of his prospective mate.

The two move continually. The cow browses and moves, browses and turns, and the attendant bull is always immediately behind her. He strokes her back and withers with his long muzzle and gently rests his head on her haunches. He repeatedly tests her readiness by sniffing and licking. When the cow moose has ovulated, the bull begins to try to mount her.

Once they have mated, a cow and bull stay near each other, eating and resting like contented old partners. At the end of their association, they part. She does not drive him away nor does he flee; they drift. At the edge of the cow's milieu, the bull noses the air with a Flehmen Response and the whole dance begins again, with another rival and another mate.

By now, autumn is a shimmering crescendo.

WINTER'S ROBE

In moose country, winter is never gone. She is an empress on sabbatical, returning to sour family picnics in July and to trouble what should be every other season's right. In gleaming alpine snowfields and in penetrating summer breezes that raise goose flesh, winter never releases her embrace; she merely loosens it a little.

In the high country, an old joke has circulated forever. One old gent asks another, "What are you going to do this summer?" And the other replies, "Well, if it comes on a Saturday, I guess I'll go fishing." So it is.

By the end of October winter has returned, reshaping the contours of the land until no memory of the bright path or sculptor's armature remains.

On cloudless days, the air is so clear and the scene so blinding white that it brings involuntary tears. And when low-pressure systems move into the valley, turgid dark clouds are like a scourge and press us flat, face first into the snow. There are cold and silence and days of little light. Perhaps most humbling is the unmitigated grace with which moose pass through this longest, meanest season.

For most of the winter, healthy moose are content and comfortable. In winter one can see how their various attributes are perfect

Adult moose can easily feed on branches nine feet or more above the ground.

adaptations to the habitat in which they live. Winter is only perceived as harsh by homo-sapiens; moose don't give it a thought.

Winter enters just as adult moose have expended tremendous energy reserves during the rut. Bulls may weigh less by 20 percent. (That would be like a 160-pound man dropping to 130 pounds in eight weeks.) Battle scars are still mending when winter comes. A cow may be carrying a calf while accompanied by her six-month-old.

Mature bull moose drop their antlers earliest of all members of the deer family, beginning in late November. Woodland Indians of northeastern and north central America believed that moose buried their antlers, which helped them explain the rarity of finding antlers.

While young spike and bi-pronged moose may have antlers through winter and shed them in early spring, most adult moose have cast them by the first of January.

The great racks are shed as the bone material diminishes between the antler base and the pedicel. When there is no longer enough support to maintain carriage of the massive appendages, they fall. There is some bleeding from the antler cavity, but the opening usually heals within hours. Late season rutting activity among bulls may result in premature antler loss.

Shed antlers deteriorate rapidly when left where they have fallen. A rich cache of calcium and mineral salts, they are eaten by mice, porcupines, squirrels and other small animals. Untouched antlers bleach white, soften and become food for soil. Triggered by the lengthening days of late winter, males begin to grow new antlers. This perfect seasonal growth-and-loss cycle enables the bull to move through deep snow without the additional weight of his antlers, and the nourishment he takes is not utilized to grow or support them.

Forage is critically important to a moose in winter. The amount and quality of forage determines whether or not a moose will survive to give birth in spring or to mate again in autumn. It determines whether or not a moose will be able to find cover, plow through deep snow or fend off predators.

The ability to find adequate forage is not controlled solely by instinct. Moose assimilate a great deal of information about the ecology and climatic conditions of their habitat. Winter can be a long, treacherous ordeal. Surviving it requires intelligence.

In the beginning of winter, moose feed primarily in riparian lowlands where willows and shrubs are abundant. However, as the snow, accumulates they may migrate to wooded slopes and plateaus, where they feed on aspen, cottonwood or birch. At higher elevations the strong branches of conifers hold or deflect huge volumes of snow, making large bowl-shaped depressions at the bases of the trees. These depressions provide protective cover and accessible forage.

The permanent but infrequent locking of antlers would result in death by starvation to both warriors.

The solitary monarch stands in silence.

Unmelted frost on a moose's coat indicates extraordinary heat-retention capabilities.

The diversity of vegetation on which moose forage is greatly diminished, and the nutritional quality of what they eat is inferior to that of spring and summer growth. This low protein, high cellulose diet is much harder for them to digest, as evidenced in their scat, which crumbles like compressed sawdust. The energy produced as a by-product of digestion is one-third less than the basal energy required for growth in summer. As if these factors were not enough, moose consume only half of what they would normally eat in August.

Moose rely in part on their fat reserves but it· is heat retention rather than heat production that is the essential element of their ability to endure winter extremes. Along with many circumpolar mammals, moose have evolved massive bodies. Their size, the insulating qualities of their pelage, and skin coloration help enable them to conserve heat. The skin of a moose is nearly black. Its nonreflective qualities absorb winter sunlight and retain generated heat.

Moose, musk-oxen and other northern animals also conserve energy by marked economy of motion. For hours at a time, completely aware, they rest. In very cold weather, any movement requires burning precious fat reserves.

The availability of good forage affects social schemes as well. Adult males seem to be the most gregarious of the sexes and age classes. In early winter, they share a friendly proximity for the first time since rut began in September. The presence of a cow experiencing a late estrus cycle may agitate the bulls temporarily into rutting behaviors, but their confrontations are much less charged than in earlier weeks.

When heavy snow falls come, good lowland forage is depleted and large groups of moose may be found within a fairly limited area. These "moose yards" have helped create the misconception that moose develop herds. Moose do not form herds. Large groups are strictly an indication of a concentration of good forage and the good sense not to get particular about close quarters. If a moose can find better forage on his own, he will do it.

There are numerous stories of moose residing in barns for the winter. One moose adopted a ranch yard late one winter and fed

companionably with horses. Another moose assumed an aggressive territorial hold on a barn and would not permit the rancher to feed his livestock.

As the season progresses, moose develop a shabby appearance that is not necessarily an indication of poor health. Their long winter pelage gradually becomes bleached and may appear light gray or white in patches. When they begin to shed their winter coats in March, the hair often falls first from their shoulders and rumps, exposing the darkly pigmented skin beneath. Lightened hair, hair that hangs in wisps, deliberate conservation of activity, and frequent and lengthy rest periods create the illusion that many moose are close to death by winter's end. In North America, predation, malnutrition and disease are the leading causes of winter deaths.

A moose makes practical use of a beaver dam to cross a frozen stream.

Moose may fall prey to a parasitic worm that attacks the brain and spinal cord, causing "moose sickness," a neurological disorder resulting in the inability of the animals to walk or carry themselves normally. Snails are the immediate host of this worm. This sickness occurs most frequently in areas of the country where moose and white-tailed deer share habitat. Unaffected by the meningeal worm, white-tailed deer pass the parasite to snails, who feed, in part, on deer droppings. Moose inadvertently ingest the snails while foraging.

The moose tick, or winter tick, is another plague. Thousands of ticks may infest one animal, causing considerable irritation. In their struggle to relieve the itching, moose will rub off large areas of hair. If hair loss is substantial, excessive heat loss may result in death.

In addition, moose are affected by many of the same diseases that affect domestic cattle, such as anthrax, brucellosis and Bang's disease.

During the Middle Ages it was believed that moose suffered from epilepsy and could cure themselves by scraping their left ear with their left hind foot until the ear bled. This left hoof was sought after because it was believed to have medicinal properties sufficient to cure humans of this malady, as well. The hoof was held in the left hand, or ground to a powder and carried in the bezel of a ring adorning the hand or applied over one's heart.

Malnutrition is probably the chief cause of mortality among moose in areas where predation is minimal; and heavy snow is probably the most common environmental factor contributing to malnutrition. When snow depths exceed chest height, movement is so labored that the moose is unable to forage successfully. Calves are the most likely to succumb to starvation. Having less fat reserve, their heat-producing capabilities are greatly reduced. Also, shorter legs force them to expend more energy when traveling through deep snow. Adults that die from malnutrition are usually aged or infirm.

Although there are exceptions, moose die, not during the harshest times when the temperatures and windchill factors are thirty or forty degrees below zero, but when the worst of winter is behind them. When the drift of spring comes in a single bird's song, they die, legs tucked beneath them, their great muzzles resting in the snow.

SANCTUARY

The night that winter came, I drove north after work. Great monolithic blue-black clouds poised on the western side of the Teton Range. There was no wind, yet a quickening in the air, a kind of friction made of ice.

No moose, where days before we'd seen half a dozen. They were down in the willows or waiting on the wooded slopes that cradle the flats. The moose knew that a change was coming. They felt the atmospheric thump of a low-pressure system. They didn't stand against it; they settled under it and waited.

At a campground, in a gentle sleeting rain I warmed tortillas over a sputtering fire. I awoke the next morning, disoriented in absolute silence, enveloped in a white parfleche. Seven inches of snow had come.

The dense quiet of these first wintry days initiates a change that comes laboriously over the next five weeks. At first the snow melts to Indian summer, then starts and halts again until finally it comes and stays.

Moose can stay an intruder with an icy glare.

The week of the first snow, the moose were in the height of rutting season. One month later the bulls, having reassembled into loose social groups, foraged near each other and sparred out of habit. I watched a weary older bull spar while kneeling. The bulls were exhausted and residual aggression was expressed with tired nudges. The big battles were over.

I felt cursed to know winter's length and tried to imagine moose thoughts. I once heard that a moose is perfectly suited to an air temperature of ten degrees Fahrenheit. Today, that was about right. My thoughts were on Annie and her dim survival statistics. Her trial would begin now. She was easier to track in the snow but she had expanded her range. From an overlook Tom and I would follow little tracks that led to the infinity of the willow flats like ellipsis points. Out among the willows we tracked her merry circles round and round. Her movements seemed urged as much by curiosity as by forage. Ten days before Thanksgiving, we lost her.

When we could not find her, we considered the possibilities. Annie might have found an adult and followed it. Continually chased by older moose, she might have sought a new refuge wherein she would not have to compete for forage. She might have followed a group of animals, taking advantage of their greater experience and ability to break snow. Annie might have succumbed.

Happily, in the first week of December, we found her southeast of her usual range. She was pursuing the companionship of a cow and male calf. When she approached the male, he lowered his ears and pretended a threatening charge. Annie pinned her ears and chased him across a snow-swept hill, where he sought safety behind his mother. The cow moose flattened her ears, lowered her head and advanced with anger that stiffened her legs. Returning the threat, Annie stood her ground and then, on second thought, sprinted away. Apparently she was asserting herself and defending her bit of territory. She was coming to know that her place in the world would be solitary.

Her sojourn lasted a few weeks before she returned to her usual range. She was alone. She seemed as comfortable as ever with our visits. We approached her openly, averting our eyes to proffer our appreciation. We frequently sat with her for more than an hour, all of us quiet and contemplative.

On the night of December 20, I was anxious about heading north the following morning; yet I needed to stand in darkness on the shortest day of the year and feel forty below and something colder with the wind, as moose did. It was insane.

Dawn seemed impossible that morning. The van was like an icy tomb. Every slow rotation of the wheels over the dry, compressed snow made a sound like ripping denim. The cold was stunning. Killing. We were speechless. Later that morning Tom's mustache froze to his beard and the casing on his camera split open with a pop. That was enough. This kind of cold etches a permanent wince in the lines of one's face. Fingernails split; hands crack and bleed unnoticed, until hours later when they throb. Breathing is shallow and cautious. Every garment is considered. Winter beats the meanness out of us like a ten-day fast. The sensations are spare, responses pure. Cold hands wrapped around a coffee mug. A heater. Better boots . . . thank you. Winter is humbling.

Open water provides respite
from deep snow.

Former rivals feed amicably together.

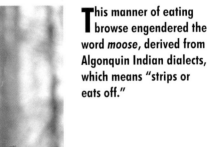

This manner of eating browse engendered the word *moose*, derived from Algonquin Indian dialects, which means "strips or eats off."

Annie rests comfortably in temperatures minus 30 degrees Fahrenheit.

The moose were fine. They were glorious. The frost lay in Carl's elegantly sculpted antlers like sugar. Instead of the more typical open-hand palmation, his antlers were like a wave at sea; they gracefully rolled and curved and were gently fluted midway up the palm.

I watched the moose and followed Annie and tried to be philosophical about all of it. But philosophy is mental generosity, and the cold took that out of me. Instead my thoughts turned in upon themselves and I tried to grasp utterly simple truths.

Unable to follow their midwinter migrations from river bottoms and marshlands into neighboring forests, we lost track of many moose whose gracious presence we had come to trust. We mused where Carl and Herk might have gone. Did Vincent go to Swan Lake? After they dropped their distinctive antlers, we would have to rely on physical markings, body sizes and on the shapes of their bells to distinguish them. Herk has a huge blanket of a bell; Carl has a bell shaped like the state of Texas. Vincent has a conspicuously notched ear. Annie is dark and small.

I saw Annie the last week of January. She lay on a slope in the protection of a wooded draw very near where we found the tiny skeleton of her sibling. She watched me and dozed intermittently. Sometimes I spoke softly to her or hummed, but I felt self-conscious and quieted myself. Although I could have and wanted to, I never touched her. I was trying not to impose a relationship with her within my human context. I felt my longing for friendship would inevitably be accompanied by expectations and that would dishonor Annie. Just to be with her—the bond between us could only be that.

Weeks went by without seeing the orphan again. We snowshoed to the brink above the flats and scanned the contrasting willows and white. Seeing no one, we lifted our chins and searched the skies for the wheeling orbits of ravens.

In February I stood at the Willow Flats overlook using a powerful spotting scope, because I could no longer risk trusting my eyes alone, nor the binoculars. I saw dark and stoic moose, motionless between bands of willow. As I looked for the orphan while knowing she would not be there, two interior halves of myself conversed: one believed and the other did not; one trusted, the other wanted proof. In March I stopped going there. I traded the vigil for the sensibilities of moose.

During the preoccupation of many weeks without seeing Annie, I snowshoed the breadth of what I had known to be her range. I stitched quilt patterns across wind-hardened lowlands, down into draws and across beaver dams. I came to know the character of my own tracks as much as those made by moose. Here I shuffled over the crust dragging the shoes; there I sank and used my splayed hands for balance.

I let go my suspicion of humans who might know of the orphan and began asking about her. Among construction workers, road crews and rangers, no one knew of her specifically, although they all had moose stories to share.

On March 1 Tom and I mustered the heart to ask two park rangers at the district office if there had been any road kills. "Only a cow elk in December so far," they said. We immediately became jovial with them and lingered in the warmth of the office to read their collage of Far Side cartoons.

We were baffled by Annie's disappearance. To our way of thinking, she should have stayed in Christian Creek, where there were cover, forage and familiar surroundings. In retrospect, the inability to find Annie sooner lay in our failure to wholly grasp her reasoning and extraordinary intelligence.

Eventually we played a hunch and discovered that Annie had migrated vertically to higher ground. She was within a half mile of her summer and fall ranges and our idiotic circles of frustration. Although we knew where she was, it was no less frustrating because we were unable to make absolute visual contact with her.

In winter moose conserve
energy by resting for long
periods of time.

To facilitate antler shedding, moose rub them against trees.

After the antler is cast there is some bleeding, but the opening heals within hours.

Her late-winter range was an idyllic place for her, and for us it was a respite from the blearing white Willow Flats. It seemed more generous and forgiving. The central topography rolled gently and supported huge fir trees combined with open areas of young lodgepole pine and shrubs. Near the brink of the windward slope, the exposed roots of conifers grew as inviting and sturdy as garden benches.

We knew Annie's track and the narrow toggle shape of her pellets. We surmised that she was remaining consistent with her behavior of staying on the periphery of another cow and calf, because adult moose tracks and the tracks of an immature moose crisscrossed hers. But we had not yet seen Annie.

Judging from her signs, sometimes she would drop off the ridge and nestle in the deep timber on its slope just before it flattened into marsh. But she would feed high. The tracks were everywhere, fresh daily.

Although the ridge was a sylvan ideal, the game of following her tracks weakened me physically and psychologically. I was jealous of Tom's long legs and muttered under my breath about it. He was always ahead and when I was tired, that mattered. Take a step, pause to wait for falling through, dig out, take another step, pause. The motion would stay in my legs and hips even after I was back at the van, on pavement sans snowshoes. I gauged happiness moment by moment and relished standing firm for a few seconds on a crusted place.

On March 17, no green save evergreen, Tom and I were back on the ridge following Annie. The trees were laden with dollops of heavy spring snow. The sound of wind in the pines was oceanic. With each rush of breeze we were wetted with the spray of flakes, then whump . . . whump, as batches of snow fell from the branches all around us.

We were following two sets of tracks that were small like Annie's, so we thought for a moment that she had passed this way twice within a short period of time. But it did not make sense, so we then reasoned that these were the tracks of a calf and small cow. We were accustomed to guesswork in our search for Annie.

Kneeling, we peeped through a cluster of young pine trees. The twosome was just twenty yards ahead of us, in dense cover. We rose slowly as they moved a few inches from shade into light. Then we saw the impossible thing; Annie and another calf.

I won't say that Annie knew us, but her scrutiny of us in that frozen moment did not indicate fear or mistrust. We stood still as trees but our hearts were twirling a joy beat. She may have sensed that.

She looked well. She looked the same. She had not grown, but even calves with mothers do not gain much weight in winter. Her coat was still dark, although the insides of her legs were lighter. Her face was still coltish, her dewlap inconsequential, and her very long mane still stood at bristling attention when wet.

Not having mastered the art of adult-moose nonchalance, Annie's friend turned, looked at us and bolted. Annie followed. They trotted effortlessly to a crescent-shaped cove of fir trees twenty yards farther. We followed them, holding our breath, trying to draw ourselves up off the creaking snow, carrying our weight in our throats. We maneuvered for a better look.

Annie's companion, taller by about six inches, was a lighter-colored female about Annie's age. She was much more suspicious and probably the orphan of a recent winterkill. The movements of the two little moose were as parallel as a dance. They stood so close that the sides of their bellies touched, and twice when they lowered their heads to sniff the pine needle mattress beneath them, their ears flicked to the feel of the other's.

From the time we met Annie, she seemed as driven by the desire for companionship as she was by the need for cover and forage. The decisions she made, based on the information she received from her environment, proved her intelligence. But her persistence at seeking companionship was beyond scientific rationale. Whether it was for security or warmth or something else entirely, it was Annie's reason.

Annie and her friend remained together through the end of winter.

TRIUMPHANT SPRING

In northern latitudes, the language of temperate zones and the seasonal reminders of calendars are useless. We fidget on the boreal shoulders of the planet and await longer light and warmer days. At the end of April, we eagerly exchange the humility wrought by winter for hope, wool for cotton, snowshoes for waders.

Our senses return like open water. Everything laps against us and we let ourselves feel again. Spring is lavish and loud, a turn and return.

In the cycle of their abbreviated migrations, moose move down out of the timbered ridges and plateaus into the willow lowlands that they love. They feed on the succulent buds of willow and ground-hugging shrubs, often kneeling to browse on delicate shoots of green grasses. They feed aggressively for hours in the blessed lengthening days.

In early spring, at his leanest, a bull moose may consume fifty pounds of forage a day to restore depleted reserves of protein and fat and to nourish antlers that have begun to grow at an enormous rate.

In spring moose replenish sodium and other minerals through tireless aquatic feeding.

In April the antlers are inconspicuous, bulbous shapes, emerging from the pedicels located about midway between the ears and eyes. The antlers grow at right angles for several inches before widening into flaring palms. During this stage of growth, the antler is extremely sensitive and delicate. For this reason, bulls are docile and eschew confrontations. If you could grasp an antler during this stage, you would feel the solidity of its understructure and the gently giving, not quite soft-as-sponge texture of the outer covering. Antlers in velvet are easily damaged. If an injury occurs to the antler structure, an odd shape or malformation may result; an injury to the pedicel will result in a permanent deformity.

Moose are shaggy in early spring. They begin to molt first over the withers, exposing the sleek jet hair of their summer coats. The process is generally complete by the middle of June.

Yearlings shed their faded beige-brown coats for darker coloration on the bodies and lighter hair on the legs.

Winter is hardest on pregnant cows, and by spring they look the worst. In the last four to six weeks before giving birth, they sacrifice to the growing fetus nearly all of the nutrition they consume. Accentuated by slim hips, their swollen bellies are most obvious when viewed from behind.

Eighty to ninety percent of females in most North American moose populations become pregnant annually. In areas of excellent unrestricted forage, a high percentage of females breed as yearlings, bear single calves, then produce twin calves as adults. Where forage is only good to average, the first breeding may be delayed a year, and there is a lower incidence of twinning. This physiological marvel—a biochemical response—enables the species to limit its population in accordance with environmental conditions.

The average gestation period is 243 days. Most infants are born during the last week of May or the first week of June. Calves born in July or early August are the offspring of a successful mating during a cow's second estrus cycle. Their chances for survival through winter are markedly reduced, because they enter winter at about half the size of a June calf.

A few weeks before the arrival of the new moose calf, a mother will spurn her yearling, rushing at him repeatedly, snorting loudly or displaying threatening postures. The astonished youngster requires several terse reminders that it is now on its own. Often, the one-year-old will remain in proximity to its mother throughout the summer, taking cues from her choices regarding forage and cover. This rejection of older offspring occurs throughout the wild realm, but it is poignant because of the richness of the bond between cow moose and their young. This is the last truly social relationship a moose will know.

When birth is imminent, the cow chooses an area of dense cover situated near water and good forage. The location must support her and the newborn for at least a week after the birth. Immediately postpartum, the cow consumes the strong-smelling afterbirth; thus the area is kept clean and predators are less likely to be attracted by the scent.

During spring snowmelt moose return to riparian lowlands that they love.

Long-legged subadults may find it easier to graze while kneeling.

Using all of their senses, moose interpret their environment with exemplary intelligence.

Calves are born with their eyes open and stand to nurse within an hour. Weighing twenty-four to thirty-five pounds, they seem as fragile as pretzel sticks. Their quavering bodies are golden, with chocolate brown circles around the eyes and on their coltish muzzles. Their survival is utterly dependent on the legendary capabilities of moose mothers.

Whereas elk form nursery herds of several females and their young to help ensure survival, moose do not need the sanctuary of a herd. Cow moose are solely responsible for their offspring. A cow moose will take on anything she considers dangerous to her calf. She will kill a perceived predator if she is able. She assesses a situation and reacts instantaneously. She is dangerous.

A mother moose is always alert. She may feed several yards from her calf, but her ears flick toward any sound. She responds with a look toward the sound and then toward her calf. Singular among the deer family, moose calves do not employ the hiding technique of pressing themselves flat; however, moose calves have been observed hiding in water, all but their noses submerged.

After three days or so, the infant is able to leave the birth area and follow its mother. To accommodate her clumsy baby, the cow's movements are deliberate and carefully chosen. She avoids difficult obstacles and hazards.

When nursing, the cow must squat to assist her baby. Later, when the calf is taller, she may nurse with one hind leg raised and extended over the calf. Nursing periods are brief, usually lasting less than a minute, and the cow determines the duration of feedings. When she is finished, she steps away.

When only days old, moose calves begin to sample tender leaves and grass. Forage combined with the rich diet of mother's milk will double a calf's weight in three weeks. During the next four months, calves will gain two pounds a day and can put on as much as five pounds per day. By October, they weigh about three hundred pounds, as much as an adult white-tailed deer.

Through coaxing and patience, a mother encourages her young to swim at an early age. When crossing rivers and rapid snow-melt streams, the cow tests the water depth by entering first, assesses the current, and then guides her youngster to enter at a place where the current will ensure its safe arrival on a sandbar or the other side. During a long swim she may tow her calf with its tiny forelegs and head resting on her rump.

It is the female moose who ensures the continuation of the species by giving birth and by passing on what she knows. She teaches her offspring survival by utilizing every sense. She demonstrates and disciplines and permits a little independence. A moose calf's bond to its mother is survival. In time, the calf responds as if a shadow. If the cow looks behind with ears erect, so does the calf.

Calves spend their days accumulating information about their world: the flight of birds, the chatter of red squirrels, the snapping of twigs. Every stimulus has meaning. Moose are born with curiosity and wonder; curiosity stays with them for life, but wonder belongs to the calves.

Moose calves are utterly
dependent on their
mothers for protection.

Nursing periods are
frequent and brief,
usually lasting less than a
minute.

The occurrence of twins is frequent in areas of plentiful food supply.

LIBERATION

In Grand Teton National Park, it seemed that every cow moose had a calf. Within a quarter-mile square, three had twins—all cinnamon-colored fur and elbows, loose jointed, gamboling babies. They moved as if controlled by an unskilled puppeteer, stepping high, tripping over clumps of nothing, walking right under Mom and out the other side of that comforting corridor. Then plop! They collapsed flat as if jerked down from beneath their little bellies.

Even in dense cover, we knew if a cow had a calf. She would quickly look behind and down, then eye us with severe consternation. Angry moose cows have been known to chase people up trees and keep them there for hours. The safety of the mother's progeny lies in her intelligence, her gut instinct and the intensity of her vigil.

The newborn moose calf has no defenses of its own. It does not have spots like the dappled light within a willow thicket. It has a scent. It does not hide as secret as a leaf upon the ground. It does not stay put while Mother wanders off on forage errands. It does not have the protection of a herd. It does not know the peril of its first days. It is utterly dependent.

Mothers move their calves often, from one safe cover to another and they prefer proximity to water. I watched cow moose move their babies in and out of shallow streams and beaver ponds, up and over riverbanks and back down again. Their movements were slow and their ways well chosen.

Water training helps ensure that the calf will be strong enough to keep up and pay attention. In this, the moose mother is also demonstrating the species' affinity for water. The calf's love for water grows in proportion to the lengthening of its legs.

Scouting for new moose one morning, we bobbled down a rutted road and, even over the sounds of the van, we heard a tremulous jingling uproar. It was the sound of thousands of spring peepers and spotted frogs just wriggled free from muddy hibernation. Their lusty racket proclaimed a readiness to mate. The sound gathered in our ears and plucked our eardrums until they found a chord that could join.

Heaped on my delight was the fact that Annie was alive, a testament to many things. She and her friend left the ridge for Annie's summer range in the second week of May. She was no longer the tiniest calf; there were infants in the fold of willows who stood thigh high to her. She was no longer the only orphan; most of the yearlings were castaways, as bewildered and dazzled as teenagers. Her behavior was so like the other youngsters that it was difficult to determine what effect not having a mother had had on Annie. For the first time since coming to know her, I could relax.

I resisted letting go in the beginning. The withdrawal from her felt like the steady strong pull of a kite in spring wind. I do not know which of us was the kite.

I watched her with her friend and other yearlings. I studied her intently, making immutable mental images of her that would endure despite the changes to come.

I see Annie, remember the enormity of her success and remember that it is done. She won't regard it at all. Annie goes on in journeys by the second, and if I am graced with the opportunity, I will look for what signifies her individuality among the tribe. And I will watch her blend into the web.

After antlers are shed in winter, new growth becomes apparent in April.

The spring molt begins first over the withers.

While antlers are in velvet bulls are docile and eschew confrontations.

Moose calves are born without spots; their mothers' vigilance precludes the necessity of camouflage.

SUMMER FEAST

In summer, the earth offers her green bounty and moose take necessary advantage. They eat and rest. But their primary interest is food. Compared with the paucity of winter forage, summer's offerings are richly varied and immediate.

Willows, leaves of cottonwood and aspen trees are favored in western ranges and paper birch and balsam firs within eastern habitats. Moose eat the tangy meadow grasses along streams and tarns while kneeling. Progressing awkwardly, they can graze in this fashion for several minutes at a time.

The essential ingredient in summer forage is salt. All mammalian bodies utilize sodium molecules to transmit electrical impulses along nerves, to maintain equilibrium within cells and to initiate the passage of compounds through membranes. It is believed that moose store excesses of sodium in the large rumen (the largest of four stomachs which contains fluids that comprise 15 percent of the total body weight). After winter, sodium reserves are radically low; the moose's physiological need for salt urges its preference for salt-rich forage, most abundant in aquatic plants. Common aquatic plants like milfoil and pondweed have salt concentrations up to four hundred times that of the woody material eaten in winter.

Virtually tireless of water food, moose frequent the still ponds and lazy backwaters that provide it. Receiving the maximum amount of nutrients while expending minimum energy, moose graze aquatic

pastures with heads submerged for up to a minute at a time. Amazingly, moose can dive nearly twenty feet for food, but generally they feed in water five feet deep or less.

Even after swims of several miles, moose show no signs of having exerted themselves. They glide up onto shore, take a wide stance and shake mightily, creating dazzling effects with light and whirling water.

Females with calves tend to feed in shallower water, with their ears above the surface. Even while feeding aggressively, a cow's ears pivot toward sounds as she assimilates the implications of the noise. The creaking of tall, swaying trees signifies only a breeze and elicits no response, but the cranky chittering of a squirrel could mean unwelcome feet in the woods. The cow jerks her head out of the water to catch an informative smell. If she suspects danger, the mother will stroll toward the shore where her resting calf waits. The oblivious calf takes advantage of a nuzzle or a snack while its mother assesses the situation and decides whether to leave the area or return to the lilies.

In summer antlers may grow an inch or more a day.

With the emergence of tines from the palm, in August antler growth is nearly complete.

Sunlight and water create a shimmering cascade.

Seeking respite from insects and heat, moose frequent backwaters and lily ponds.

During the short summer, moose calves transform. Their coats change from a honey color to a reddish chestnut and finally to the rich, dark color of adults. Faces broaden, necks lengthen and by the end of August, the dark circles around the eyes are gone and the insides of the legs have lightened to an ash-blond color.

Calves are weaned before the rut begins, when mothers will be too preoccupied to indulge suckling. Weaning seems to be gradual and uneventful. The calf seems neither bewildered by this nor insistent.

In summer adult bulls are the most diligent feeders and concentrate in areas of good forage for days at a time. With the nutritional demands of growing antlers, bulls consume 50 percent more food than they actually need. The excess is stored as fat and muscle tissues which will empower them through the rut, when they eat little, and sustain them through winter, when less is available to eat.

Groups of bulls may forage together, but for the most part they ignore one another. When territorial disputes occur, bulls may vocalize with rough snorts or even charge a short distance, but there is rarely contact. This is because of the painful delicacy of their growing antlers. Velvet is easily bruised and bleeds freely if lacerated. Bruises appear as whitish marks and remain on the antler as long as it is in velvet.

Peak antler growth seems to coincide with the length of daylight. An average bull moose with an antler spread of four feet will grow antlers at the rate of one-and-a-half inches per day. One can imagine them unfurling like broad-leafed philodendrons.

In summer, if adult moose are not eating or on their way to eating, they are resting. When the alpine sun is at its highest, moose retire to cool glades and shadowy timbered areas; with their relaxed demeanor they embody summertime bliss. Swishing their ears to scatter black flies into whips of flight, they sigh and yawn and each breath slightly rocks their great heads. Reclining moose may rest their heads along their flanks, or in a lowered position cushion their muzzles on one or both forelegs. Their eyes are closed for only a few minutes at a time, and there are few intervals when moose are not ruminating the morning's forage. After a time, they stretch with stiffened vibrato, forelegs extended, necks arched, followed by a little shake of the head and mane. Then with a see-saw-off-its-hinge action, they stand. They munch obligatorily for a few seconds and then lie down on their opposite side.

The duration of the feeding and resting cycle is a matter of individual needs and preferences. Generally, the species eats with greatest intensity in the still, cool hours of dawn and dusk and rests during the sun's long zenith. On hot days, moose may rest standing belly deep in water or lie in the shallows. Unfailingly they seek shade.

In the evenings of mid-August, a portentous chill comes. In early morning hours frost steals across lowlands. Summer begins to weaken while adult moose are at their fittest.

Moose are excellent
swimmers.

As summer ends, calves take on the countenance and coloration of adults.

With their prehensile upper lip, moose feel for the roots and tubers of favorite aquatic plants.

Responding to a vaguely mounting sexual drive, bulls become more restless. They may continue to feed within sight of each other, but the margins of intolerance expand. When antlers are joined it is with concentration and reserve.

Adults of both sexes seem particularly impatient with the antics of accompanying yearlings. Often, yearling bulls seek the company of elder bulls and test themselves through playful imitations. Due to the increased forage demands on a given range, territorial behaviors of cow moose intensify. By now, the four-month-old moose calf is eating the same foods as its mother and weaning is nearly complete.

It is nearly the culmination: a show-stopper staged at the beginning. Moose vibrate in this time like guitar strings stretched tighter and tighter until sprung. If we could perch like finches on the wires of moose life, we would anticipate everything, fear nothing and regret nothing, not even the fleeting of summer.

EPILOGUE

Even though I have been with the moose through the cycle of a whole year, I am still looking. Looking requires some skill, a wrestling with the eyes wanting to travel quickly over the terrain, a reptilian sensitivity to heat, and a wild thing's suspicion of movement. Earnestly looking for moose, or anything, takes some courage, because the purpose—which is to actually see—can change one forever.

This morning I saw Annie. She was traveling quickly along the base of a timbered ridge at the edge of Willow Flats. Her coat reflected the early sun and her dun-colored legs vanished from view in the tall, dry grass of autumn. She moved with such speed and grace that I was struck by the economy of her gait; she could probably balance a teacup on her flat back while trotting. I recognized the bristle of her mane, her tuft of dewlap, and the profile of her head held high; but it was her apparent determination that identified her as much as anything.

When I caught up, I saw that Annie thought she had located potential friends: another cow and calf. The older cow was utterly confounded by Annie's insistent accompaniment and repeatedly vocalized her disapproval. The three moose churned like an eddy within the small clearing. Annie frolicked to and from the cow, and the cow sprinted this way and that, wild-eyed, shaking her head and stomping her forelegs.

Increasingly irritable, bulls thrash the brush and hone antlers in prelude to the rut.

Antlers in velvet are exceedingly fragile and bruises appear as white marks.

With its calf resting nearby, a cow moose remains alert to sounds while feeding in shallow water.

A cow moose inspects the antlers of a prospective swain.

In the past, Annie's behavior has been awkward enough, with only forage at stake, but now she poses an additional threat. It is rutting season and the orphan seems uninterested in playing a part. This is her second autumn, and although she is smaller than other cows—and will always be—Annie is mature enough to mate. It could happen later this season. When Annie bears a calf she will no longer be an outsider. I wonder who she will choose to court her.

Through binoculars I spotted Vincent in a northwestern portion of the flats. I consider him the most venerable of the boys. The silvery coloration and horizontal markings over the bridge of his muzzle give him a look of wisdom and age. In some years, long shreds of velvet hang from his antlers into October, evidence that he has remained unchallenged. In fact, the only other bull that could suitably challenge Vincent is Carl; the two are equally matched in size and apparent strength. Carl reigns in the south and southwestern areas of the Willow Flats, where he is regarded with deference by all others. He wields an icy, penetrating stare as effectively as he does his massive antlers. With his comportment of severity and majesty, he is fearsome. For many years, Carl and Vincent have been archetypical lords over the marsh.

From my seated perch, I longed to see the boys standing together so that I could compare how well they wear autumn. But each had his own section of the flats, each was moving urgently as if being directed to his place on stage, before the curtain. One of the acts that would ensue would be the old rivalry between Herkimer and Victor, two bulls in their prime.

I will never forget their fierce battle on an autumn morning last year during a storm. Lightning flashed and sounded simultaneously at half-minute intervals, and the combination of dense air and eerie light lent an ominous magic to a spectacular fight between the two. The titanic force of their repeated crashes reverberated through the willows for nearly an hour, and in the end, Herkimer was bleeding from a puncture in his chest and both bulls were exhausted. They dropped their heads, gasping deeply for air, in what seemed like a choreographed acknowledgement of each other and the partaken ritual. Finally Herkimer retreated, disappearing into the maze. Victor retired to a shallow beaver pond where he drank intensely. Within moments he was joined by the cow for whom all had been demonstrated.

I came north this morning to see moose, hoping to touch base with reality and to sense the continuity and scale of our mutual destinies. I have never been disappointed. I did not see any dramatic culminations among fellows like Herkimer and Victor, but I saw Annie. What is more, when Annie saw me, she paused for a good, long look.

A moose creates a whirling shower of water as she shakes her great head.